**W9-CBZ-147**

# IGUANODON

## AND OTHER SPIKY-THUMBED PLANT-EATERS

# Prehistoric World

# IGUANODON

# AND OTHER SPIKY-THUMBED PLANT-EATERS

## VIRGINIA SCHOMP

**Marshall Cavendish**
Benchmark

New York

# Contents

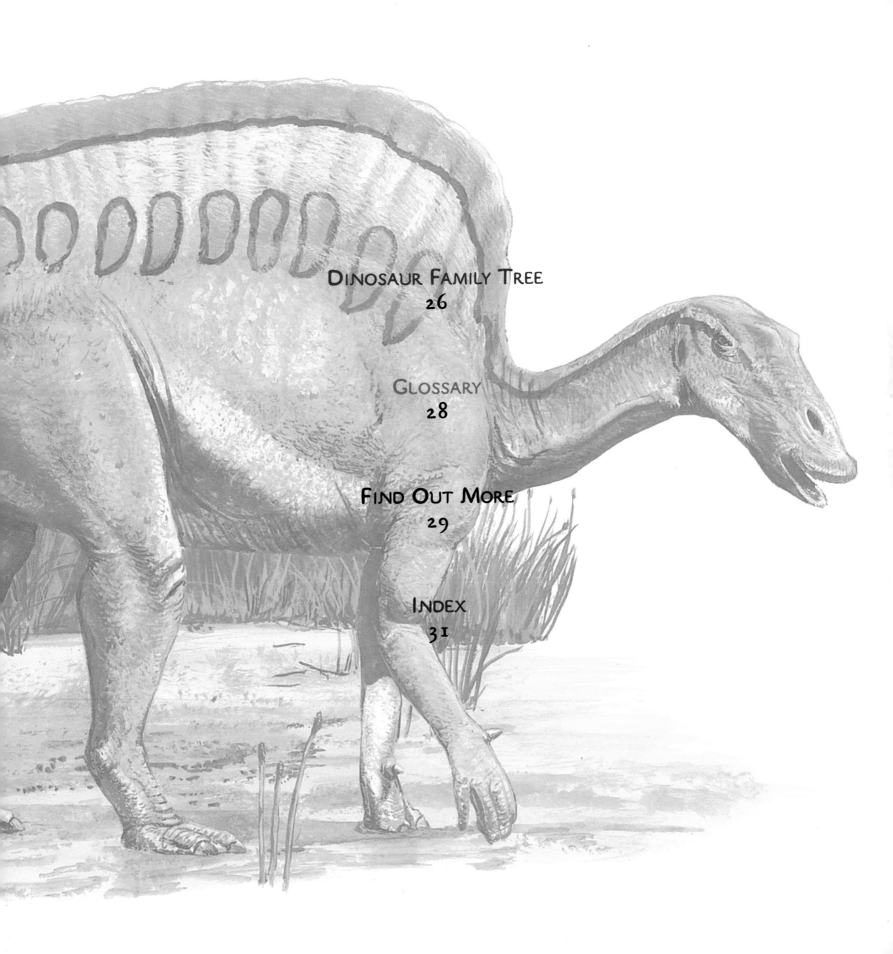

# HANDY THUMB SPIKES

A herd of *Iguanodon* moves across a vast green plain. One of the dinosaurs stops to munch on some ferns. That tasty snack is nearly its last meal! A fierce meat-eating dinosaur has been stalking the herd. Spotting the lone plant-eater, the hunter attacks. The *Iguanodon* bellows in alarm. Rearing up on its hind legs, it lashes out with its arms. Instead of thumbs, the *Iguanodon* has a long sharp spike on each hand. One of those thumb spikes stabs the meat-eater's neck. Now it is the hunter's turn to howl, while the *Iguanodon* races back to the safety of the herd.

*An* Iguanodon *uses its sharp thumb spike to fight off a fierce meat-eating dinosaur.*

*Iguanodon* belonged to a large group of plant-eating dinosaurs called ornithopods. The word "ornithopod" means "bird foot." When these dinosaurs walked on their hind legs, they left three-toed footprints like the tracks made by birds.

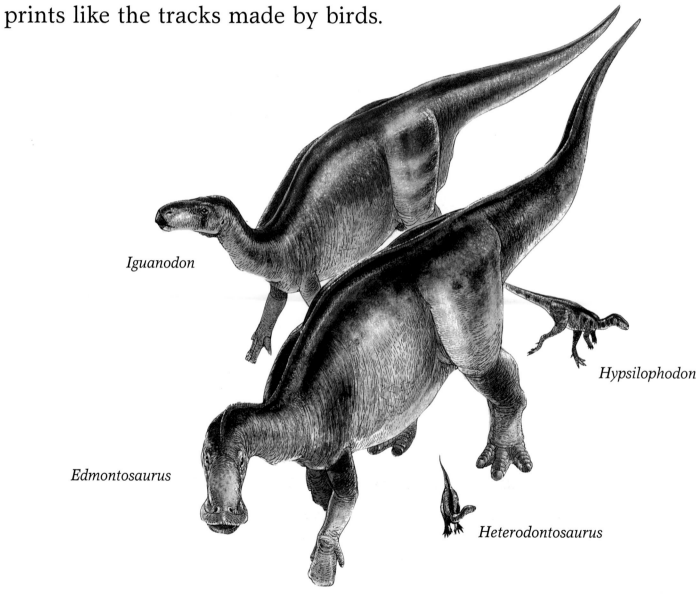

*Iguanodon*

*Hypsilophodon*

*Edmontosaurus*

*Heterodontosaurus*

*Ornithopods were plant-eating dinosaurs that could walk on either two or four legs. They came in many sizes, from three-foot-long* Heterodontosaurus *to massive* Edmontosaurus, *as long as a bus.*

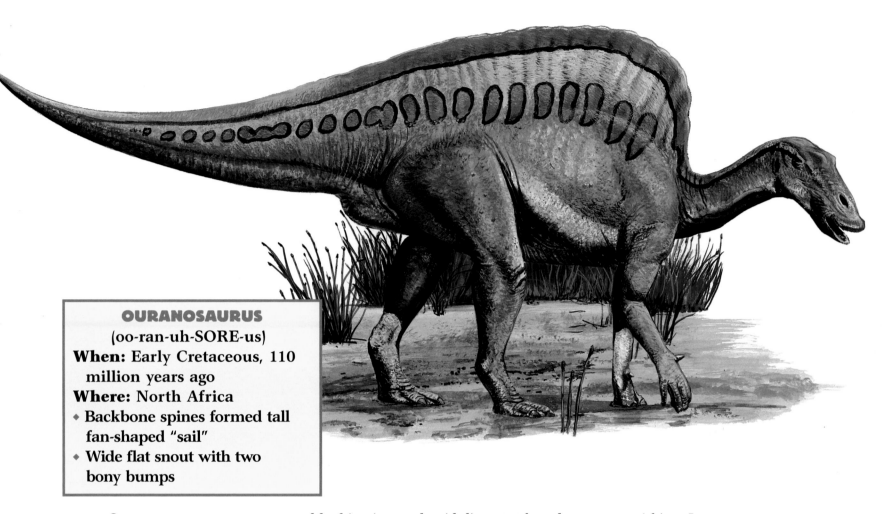

Ouranosaurus *was an unusual-looking iguanodontid dinosaur from hot, steamy Africa. It may have used the skin-covered "sail" on its back to regulate its body temperature, turning to let the sail catch the sun or the cooling breezes.*

Paleontologists (scientists who study prehistoric life) have divided the ornithopods into several smaller groups, or families. The iguanodontid family included large ornithopods with hard toothless beaks, rows of cheek teeth, and a spiked thumb on each hand. The chart on page 26 shows how these handy plant-eaters fit into the dinosaur family tree.

## HEAD OF THE FAMILY

The iguanodontid family was named for its largest and best-known member, *Iguanodon*. This giant was longer than a fire engine and as heavy as an elephant. It had a long stiff tail and a bony beak. About one hundred strong teeth lined the sides of its mouth.

*This fossil of an* Iguanodon *foot shows the dinosaur's three long clawed toes.*

*Iguanodon could walk on two legs or on all fours. When it stood on its hind legs, its long outstretched tail helped the dinosaur keep its balance.*

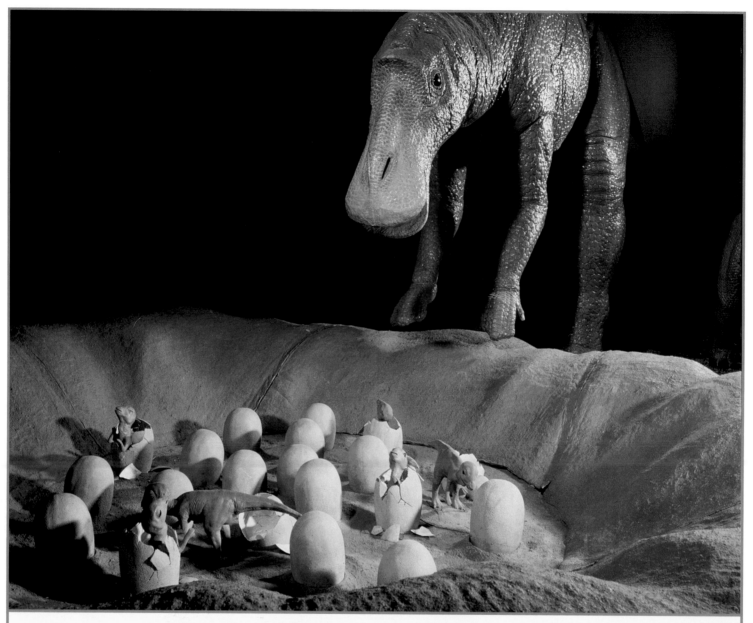

## BRINGING UP BABY

Like all dinosaurs, *Iguanodon* hatched from eggs. However, no fossils of *Iguanodon* nests or babies have yet been found. To figure out how these dinosaurs raised their young, paleontologists must study evidence left by other ornithopods.

*Maiasaura* was an ornithopod closely related to *Iguanodon*. Studies of its fossil nests show that parents probably took good care of their hatchlings. In the model pictured above, a mother *Maiasaura* is watching over her babies. She will feed and protect them until they are ready to leave the nest and take their place in the dinosaur herd.

*Iguanodon*'s arms were shorter and thinner than its legs. It had very unusual hands. The dinosaur's three middle fingers ended in small flattened hooves. Its "pinky" finger could be curled across the palm to grasp objects. Its long bony thumb spike stuck out sideways from its hand like a permanent "thumbs-up" sign. *Iguanodon* probably used its multipurpose hands for walking, gathering food, and defending itself against the fierce predators of the dinosaur world.

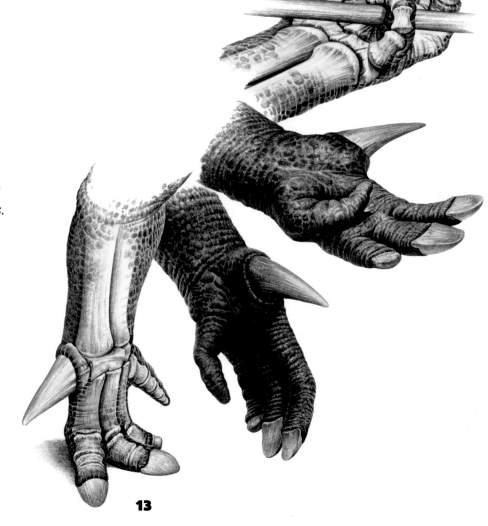

Iguanodon *had four fingers and a thumb spike. Its remarkable hands could be used for a variety of tasks.*

# IGUANODON'S WORLD

The first *Iguanodon* appeared about 135 million years ago, at the beginning of the Cretaceous period. During that long-ago stretch of time, the earth's landmasses were closer together than they are today. In some parts of the world, animals could walk from one continent to another. *Iguanodon* spread to every continent except Antarctica. Paleontologists have found its fossils in many different places, especially Belgium, England, Germany, North Africa, and the United States.

## The Age of Dinosaurs

*Dinosaurs walked the earth during the Mesozoic era, also known as the Age of Dinosaurs. The Mesozoic era lasted from about 250 million to 65 million years ago. It is divided into three periods: Triassic, Jurassic, and Cretaceous. (Note: In the chart, MYA stands for "million years ago.")*

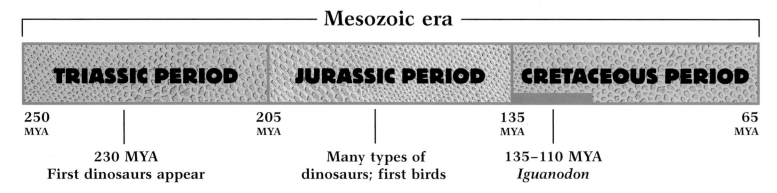

Mesozoic era

| TRIASSIC PERIOD | JURASSIC PERIOD | CRETACEOUS PERIOD |
|---|---|---|

| 250 MYA | 205 MYA | 135 MYA | 65 MYA |

230 MYA
First dinosaurs appear

Many types of
dinosaurs; first birds

135–110 MYA
*Iguanodon*

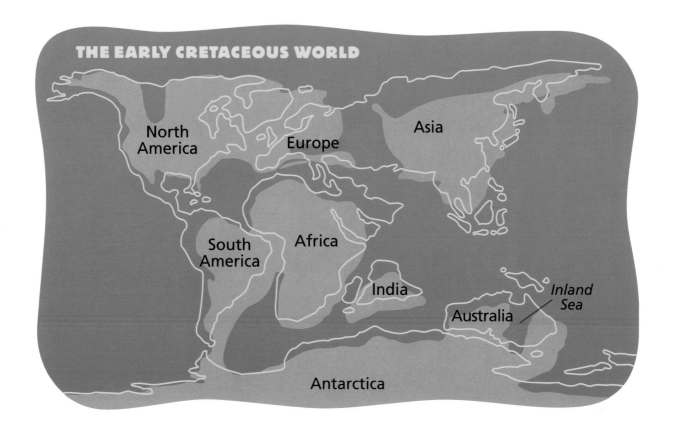

THE EARLY CRETACEOUS WORLD

*The face of the earth is always changing, as the continents slowly move. The yellow outlines on the map show the shape of the modern continents. The green shading shows their position about 135 million years ago, in the days of* Iguanodon.

## PLANT-EATERS AND PREDATORS

Let's take a trip back to the Early Cretaceous period. Our time machine lands in what will one day be southern England. The air feels warm and damp. Trees, shrubs, and ferns stretch for miles. Sprinkled across this vast green-and-brown carpet are tiny spots of color. The world's first flowering plants have just begun to bloom.

Many different dinosaurs move across this prehistoric landscape. We might see groups of *Iguanodon* and other plant-eaters. Small two-legged dinosaurs nibble on the ferns, while long-necked giants gobble up the treetops. Armored plant-eaters plod along on four legs, shielded by the bony spikes on their backs.

Polacanthus *was an armored plant-eater that sometimes mingled with* Iguanodon *herds. It had a good sense of smell, and* Iguanodon *had good hearing and eyesight, so the two dinosaurs could have helped each other watch out for predators.*

Wherever there are plant-eaters, there are sure to be predators eager to eat them! One of the scariest-looking meat-eaters of *Iguanodon*'s world is *Baryonyx*. Some paleontologists believe that this two-ton terror mainly ate fish. Others think that *Baryonyx* could have used its foot-long claws to hunt and kill other dinosaurs.

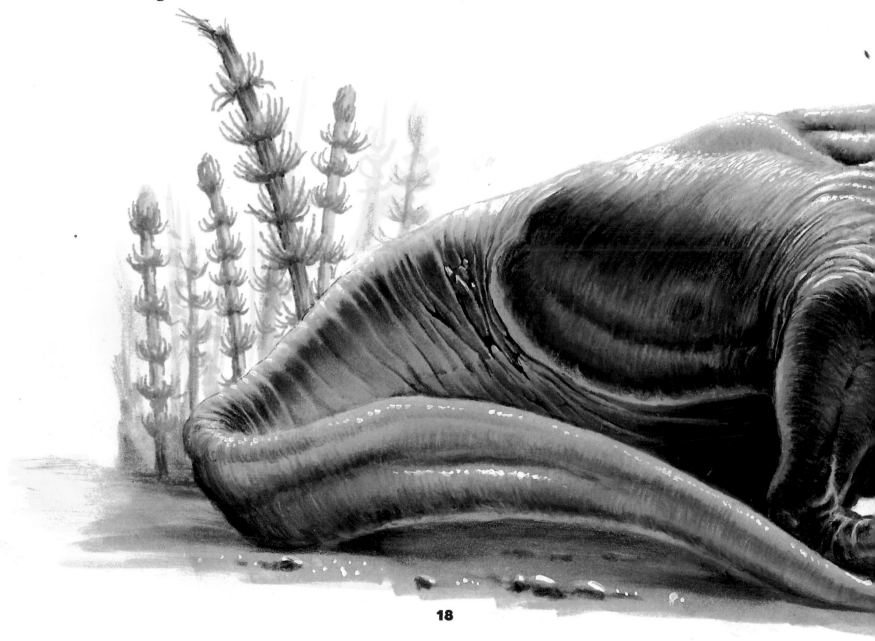

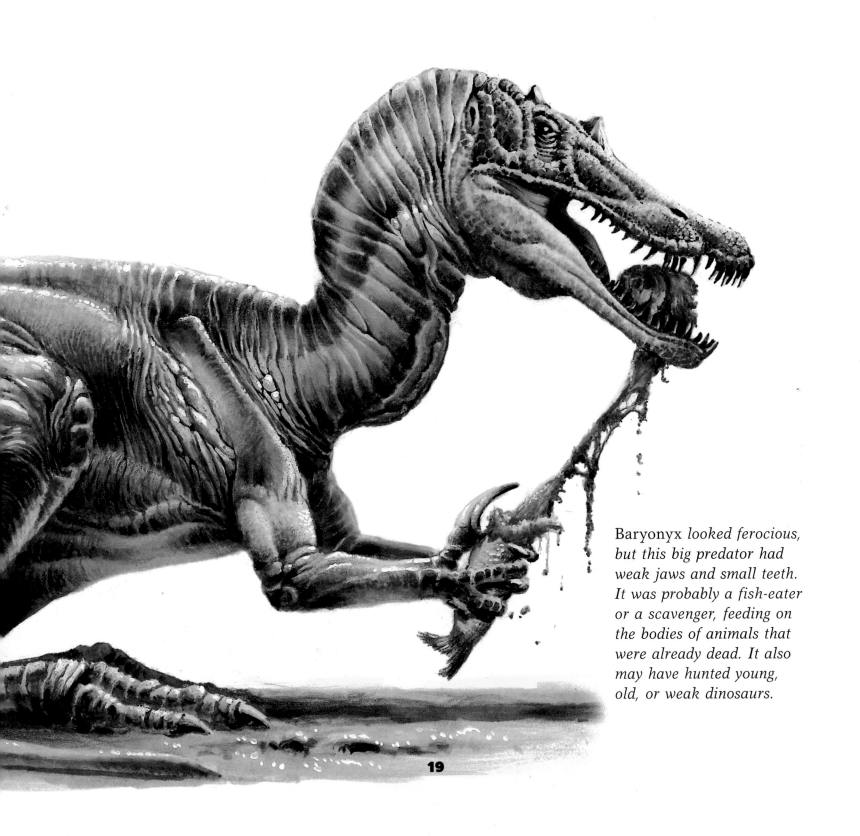

Baryonyx looked ferocious, but this big predator had weak jaws and small teeth. It was probably a fish-eater or a scavenger, feeding on the bodies of animals that were already dead. It also may have hunted young, old, or weak dinosaurs.

19

# LIFE IN A CROWD

**M**any paleontologists believe that *Iguanodon* lived together in herds for protection from predators. The dinosaurs probably spent most of their time eating. Walking around slowly on all fours, they searched for low-growing plants. Full-grown adults could rise up on their hind legs to reach branches sixteen feet above the ground.

*Iguanodon* was one of the first dinosaurs to chew its food. It chopped off twigs, leaves, and other pieces of plants with its hard, toothless beak. Then it ground the tough meal to a pulp with its strong cheek teeth.

*Like its bigger cousin* Iguanodon, Rhabdodon *probably traveled in small herds. Living in a group meant that there were always many eyes and ears on the alert for dangerous predators.*

**RHABDODON**
(RAB-duh-don)
**When:** Late Cretaceous,
70–65 million years ago
**Where:** western Europe
◆ Last known iguanodontid
◆ Weighed only 1,000
pounds—about as much
as a polar bear

Few predators would dare to attack a herd of three-ton *Iguanodon*. If one of the plant-eaters *was* threatened, it might just run away. An adult *Iguanodon* probably could run about twelve miles an hour on its hind legs. Not fast enough? The dinosaur could always use its "secret weapon"—its daggerlike thumb spikes.

**TENONTOSAURUS**
(teh-non-tuh-SORE-us)
**When:** Early Cretaceous,
120–100 million years ago
**Where:** North America
- Primitive (less developed) relative of *Iguanodon*
- Tail much longer than the rest of the body

Tenontosaurus *was a primitive iguanodontid with a toothless beak and lots of cheek teeth, but no thumb spikes.*

# THE END OF *IGUANODON*

In the middle of the Cretaceous period, new trees and plants with tougher bark, stems, and leaves began to grow. A new group of plant-eaters also appeared. These were the hadrosaurs, or duck-billed dinosaurs.

The duckbills had hundreds of extra-strong teeth, which were constantly replaced as they wore down. That made these dinosaurs much better than the iguanodontids at grinding up tough plants. In most parts of the world, *Iguanodon* and its relatives slowly died out, and the duckbills took over their old feeding grounds. These champion chewers would flourish right up to the end of the Age of Dinosaurs.

*Some paleontologists think that* Probactrosaurus *was a link between the* Iguanodon-*like dinosaurs and their descendants, the duckbills. About 65 million years ago, the duckbills and all the other remaining dinosaurs died out.*

**PROBACTROSAURUS**
(pro-back-truh-SORE-us)
**When:** Early Cretaceous,
100 million years ago
**Where:** China and
Mongolia
◆ Features of both
iguanodontids and
duck-billed dinosaurs
◆ Only incomplete fossils
have been found

# Dinosaur Family Tree

**ORDER**

All dinosaurs are divided into two large groups, based on the shape and position of their hip bones. Ornithischians had backward-pointing hip bones, like birds.

**SUBORDER**

Ornithopods were plant-eaters that could walk on two or four legs. They had birdlike feet, beaks, and stiff tails.

**INFRAORDER**

Iguanodontians were a widespread group of ornithopods, ranging in size from small to very large plant-eaters.

**FAMILY**

A family includes one or more types of closely related dinosaurs. The iguanodontid family included large spiky-thumbed plant-eaters.

**GENUS**

Every dinosaur has a two-word name. The first word tells us what genus, or type, of dinosaur it is. The genus plus the second word are its species—the group of very similar animals it belongs to. (For example, *Iguanodon bernissartensis* is one species of *Iguanodon*.)

Scientists organize all living things into groups, according to features shared.
This chart shows one way of grouping the spiky-thumbed plant-eaters in this book.

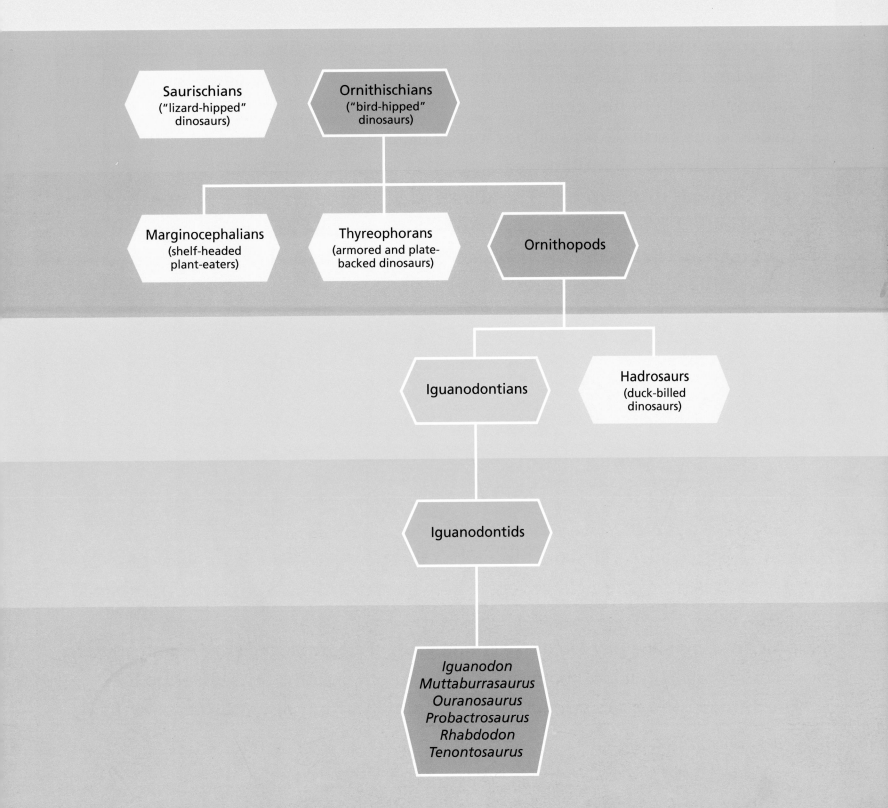

Saurischians
("lizard-hipped"
dinosaurs)

Ornithischians
("bird-hipped"
dinosaurs)

Marginocephalians
(shelf-headed
plant-eaters)

Thyreophorans
(armored and plate-
backed dinosaurs)

Ornithopods

Iguanodontians

Hadrosaurs
(duck-billed
dinosaurs)

Iguanodontids

*Iguanodon*
*Muttaburrasaurus*
*Ouranosaurus*
*Probactrosaurus*
*Rhabdodon*
*Tenontosaurus*

# Glossary

**Baryonyx** (bah-ree-ON-iks): *Baryonyx* was a meat-eating dinosaur that lived in England about 125 million years ago. It had a long crocodile-like snout and many small pointed teeth.

**Cretaceous** (krih-TAY-shus) **period:** The Cretaceous period lasted from about 135 million to 65 million years ago.

**duck-billed dinosaurs:** The duck-billed dinosaurs were plant-eaters that descended from the iguanodontids and became the most common land animals on Earth during the Late Cretaceous period. They are also called duckbills or hadrosaurs.

**fossils:** Fossils are the hardened remains or traces of animals or plants that lived many thousands or millions of years ago.

**iguanodontid** (ig-wahn-uh-DON-tid): The iguanodontid family of dinosaurs included large plant-eaters such as *Iguanodon*. Iguanodontids had toothless beaks, cheek teeth, and a bulky tail. Most members of the family also had a thumb spike on each hand.

**Maiasaura** (mie-uh-SORE-uh): *Maiasaura* was a duck-billed dinosaur from the Late Cretaceous period.

**ornithopods** (or-NITH-uh-pods): Ornithopods were plant-eating dinosaurs that could walk on two or four legs. Their footprints looked like the tracks made by birds.

**paleontologists** (pay-lee-on-TAH-luh-jists): Paleontologists are scientists who study fossils to learn about dinosaurs and other forms of prehistoric life.

**predators:** Predators are animals that hunt and kill other animals for food.

# Find Out More

## Books

Cohen, Daniel. *Iguanodon*. Mankato, MN: Capstone Press, 2003.

Cole, Stephen. *Walking with Dinosaurs: Photo Journal*. New York: Dorling Kindersley, 2000.

Fritz, Sandy, and George Olshevsky. *Iguanodon*. Discovering Dinosaurs series. North Mankato, MN: Smart Apple Media, 2003.

Gray, Susan H. *Iguanodon*. Exploring Dinosaurs series. Chanhassen, MN: Child's World, 2004.

Hartzog, Brooke. *Iguanodon and Dr. Gideon Mantell*. Dinosaurs and Their Discoverers series. New York: PowerKids Press, 1999.

Holmes, Thom, and Laurie Holmes. *Peaceful Plant-Eating Dinosaurs: The Iguanodonts, Duckbills, and Other Ornithopods*. Berkeley Heights, NJ: Enslow Publishers, 2001.

Kerley, Barbara. *The Dinosaurs of Waterhouse Hawkins*. New York: Scholastic Press, 2001.

Marshall, Chris, ed. *Dinosaurs of the World*. 11 volumes. New York: Marshall Cavendish, 1999.

Matthews, Rupert. *Iguanodon*. Gone Forever series. Chicago, IL: Heinemann Library, 2003.

Parker, Steve. *The Ornithopods*. Volume 7, *The Age of the Dinosaurs*. Danbury, CT: Grolier Educational, 2000.

# ONLINE SOURCES *

***Dino Directory*** at **http://internt.nhm.ac.uk/jdsml/dino**
The Natural History Museum in London, England, presents this guide to more than one hundred dinosaurs. There are facts and photos from museum exhibits featuring several spiky-thumbed plant-eaters, including *Iguanodon*.

***Iguanodon 1822 to Present Day: The Changing Shape of a Dinosaur*** at **http://www.dinohunters.com/Iguanodon/iggy%20index.htm**
Words and photos tell the story of *Iguanodon*'s discovery and the different ways scientists have reconstructed the dinosaur, from early drawings through modern-day robots.

***Jurassic Park Institute*** at **http://www.jpinstitute.com/index.jsp**
Created by Universal Studios, this entertaining Web site offers lots of information for dinosaur fans. You can investigate eggs and nests in the "Dino Lab" and print out dinosaur trading cards in "Dinopedia."

***Royal Belgian Institute of Natural Sciences*** at **http://euromin.w3sites.net/Nouveau_site/musees/bruxelles/MUSBRUe.htm**
Belgium's Museum of Natural History houses about thirty nearly complete *Iguanodon* skeletons discovered in a coal mine in the village of Bernissart. Click on the link in "The Iguanodons of Bernissart" for a photograph of this famous exhibit.

***Walking with Dinosaurs*** at **http://www.bbc.co.uk/dinosaurs**
This companion site to the BBC television series *Walking with Dinosaurs* presents in-depth information on more than sixty dinosaurs through sound, video, photographs, and interactive games. Click on "Fact Files" for movie clips of *Iguanodon*'s cousin *Muttaburrasaurus*.

*Web site addresses sometimes change. The addresses here were all available when this book was sent to press. For more online sources, check with the media specialist at your local library.

# Index

## About the Author

Virginia Schomp grew up in a quiet suburban town in northeastern New Jersey where eight-ton duck-billed dinosaurs once roamed. In first grade, she discovered that she loved reading and writing, and in sixth grade she was voted "class bookworm," because she always had her nose in a book. Today she is a freelance writer who has published more than fifty books for young readers on topics including animals, careers, American history, and ancient cultures. Ms. Schomp lives in the Catskill Mountain region of New York State with her husband, Richard, and their son, Chip.

Dinosaurs lived millions of years ago. Everything we know about them—how they looked, walked, ate, fought, mated, and raised their young—comes from educated guesses by the scientists who discover and study fossils. The information in this book is based on what most scientists believe right now. Tomorrow or next week or next year, new discoveries could lead to new ideas. So keep your eyes and ears open for news flashes from the prehistoric world!

Marshall Cavendish Benchmark
99 White Plains Road
Tarrytown, New York 10591-9001
www.marshallcavendish.us

Text copyright © 2006 by Marshall Cavendish Corporation
Map copyright © 2006 by Marshall Cavendish Corporation
Map and Dinosaur Family Tree by Robert Romagnoli

Library of Congress Cataloging-in-Publication Data

Schomp, Virginia.
Iguanodon : and other spiky-thumbed plant-eaters / by Virginia Schomp.
p. cm. — (Prehistoric world)
Includes bibliographical references and index.
Summary: "Describes the physical characteristics and behavior of Iguanodon
and other spiky-thumbed plant-eaters"—Provided by publisher.
ISBN 0-7614-2005-3
1. Iguanodon—Juvenile literature. 2. Dinosaurs—Juvenile literature.
I. Title. II. Series.

QE862.O65S42 2005
567.912—dc22

2004027742

Front and back cover illustrations by John Sibbick

The illustrations and photographs in this book are used by permission and through the courtesy of
*Marshall Cavendish Corporation:* 2-3, 4-5, 8, 9, 11, 15, 16-17, 18-19, 20-21, 22-23, 25;
*John Sibbick:* 7, 13; *Natural History Museum Photo Library, London:* 10, 12.

Printed in China

1 3 5 6 4 2